Praise for Cameron Morse:

Father Me Again explores the bittersweet complications of being simultaneously an expectant father and a glioblastoma patient, which is itself a contrary kind of expectancy. Stretched between diametric life events, oscillating between oncology treatments and prenatal care appointments, Cameron Morse has no option but to grapple with the dark side of hope, to flail in a preternatural web of uncertainty, and to ultimately find redemption by learning to *Sing and singe in the threadbare seam / between being and being gone.* This book will have you thanking it for breaking your heart.

—Jessica Goodfellow, author of *Whiteout.*

Cameron Morse deftly handles the big themes—birth, love, mortality—and well knows *the thumb of God* pressing down on him; but these poems grow in stature and distinction by elevating seemingly mundane details of life. Instead of listening only, and merely, to God's voice in the wind, Morse says, *I hear / a hiss in the oak leaves / like rice pouring into an empty pot.* Such stunning imagery allows us readers to live more intensely. The generational vitality that celebrates a new son and laments a missing father, for example, finds language that is both human and steady: *But Dad,* says the poet, *If you aren't / coming, I will take your place.* Cameron Morse is a gifted poet, whose poems are a gift to the rest of us.

—Robert Stewart, author of *Working Class.*

Cameron Morse's *Father Me Again* is, yes, a meditation on earthly and heavenly fathers and sons, but it is also an in-the-moment journal of the poet's encounter with brain cancer. Poems in this collection are carefully crafted; imagery is one of the poet's special gifts. Despite—or, perhaps, in service to—his preternatural themes, Morse's poems most often begin in the quotidian, *The interstate tosses / in its rocky bed, all the contrivances / of man. Oak leaves choke / the storm drain. No one is coming / to clean up the mess*—and, almost always confront spiritual, personal and familial quandaries. *Father Me Again* is an extraordinary, honest reckoning of the human condition.

> —Jeanetta Calhoun Mish, 2017-18 Oklahoma State Poet Laureate, author of *What I Learned at the War*

These are remarkable poems, as brave as poems can ever be. Their hallmark is their balanced sensitivity and strength, each rendered with such clarity as to make each poem a singular achievement. They chronicle what Morse calls *this narrow life,* this transition we all are making between life and death, but which he sees with an intensity few of us will ever know. His life is peopled with an absent father, an extraordinary wife, a beloved son, and all the host of heavens that is the natural world, which he sees fiercely, fully, as *strings of geese draped overhead like prayer beads,* and as he vows courageously to *sing and singe in the threadbare seam between being and being gone.* He knows his life is not his own, and yet it is, when he reaches to hold his wife's hand, when his son's eyes meet his and are his, and when his son says *Oh,* when Morse is reading to him and they both fill up with perfect joy. Readers of these poems will react the same way and fill with that same understanding.

> —John Hodgen, author of *Grace.*

Cameron Morse is poet, like Rilke, who writes so widely and alertly in the midst of our mortal panorama—not around it, or in spite of it, or approximately near it: *Sing and singe in the threadbare seam between being and being gone.* These are poems that confront both time and timelessness, until these states merge into one unified pitch of nearness and nowness and here. Morse's poems demonstrate intimacy's élan vital of interdependence and spaciousness, and he knows that to live one must remain continually intimate, so as to unify one's hidden inwardness with the outward, exquisite field of the world. To do this, which so many of us fail to do, is what's otherwise known as love.

—Jordan Stempleman, author of *Wallop*.

If everything in Father Me Again is bereaved and estranged, it is also newborn. When Morse *speaks* his *shriek*, he does so *among the living,* and he does not muzzle his wonderment. What a joy to stumble headlong into poems of such equipoise, what anguish, what solace.

—L. S. Klatt, *The Wilderness After Which*.

Father Me Again

≈ poems ≈

Cameron Morse

Kansas City   Spartan Press   Missouri

Spartan Press
Kansas City, Missouri
spartanpresskc.com

Copyright (c) Cameron Morse, 2018
First Edition 1 3 5 7 9 10 8 6 4 2
ISBN: 978-1-946642-58-5
LCCN: 2018949518

Design, edits and layout: Jason Ryberg
Cover image and author photo: Li Ni
All rights reserved. No part of this publication may be reproduced or transmitted in any form or by any means, electronic or mechanical, including photocopying, recording or by info retrieval system, without prior written permission from the author.

Spartan Press would like to thank Prospero's Books, The Fellowship of N-finite Jest, The Prospero Institute of Disquieted P/o/e/t/i/c/s, Will Leathem, Tom Wayne, Jeanette Powers, j. d. tulloch, Jon Bidwell, Jason Preu, Mark McClane, Tony Hayden and the whole Osage Arts Community.

I am grateful to my wife, Lili—who stands at the center of this collection—my son Theodore, may you one day learn to read! I would also like to thank Mom, Aunt Cathi and Cousin Bryce, for getting me to class on time. For help with my manuscript, I am indebted to Max McBride, Diane Glancy, and my thesis committee: Robert Stewart, Hadara Bar-Nadav and John Barton; and to my workshop at Inklings' Books and Coffee Shoppe: Eve Brackenbury, Ariel Diaz, K.L. Frank, and Jemshed Khan. I am also grateful to the editors in whose magazines the following poems first appeared (some in earlier forms):

Algebra of Owls: "Requiem for Heavenly Mountain Road." *Evening Street Review*: "Poem Written During a Funeral Service." *Fourth & Sycamore:* "Timetables." *From Sac:* "Easter Sunday." *Gravel:* "Grasp Reflex," "Hives," "Mansions." *I-70 Review:* "Praying Mantis." *Into the Void:* "Rain on the Fourth of July." *Kawsmouth:* "Unwritten Letter," "At the Independence Women's Clinic." *The Lark:* "At the KU Cancer Center." *Leaping Clear:* "Waiting." *The Literary Nest:* "Rooming In," "SIDS." *Madcap Review*: "Fathers." *Mascara Review:* "Apnea." *Mocking Heart Review:* "Halloween." *Neologism:* "Crickets." *New Madrid: a Journal of Contemporary Literature:* "Voices," "Corona." *Nude Bruce:* "Housefly." *Papercuts:* "Going Ahead." *Parentheses Journal:* "Wind Chill." The *Portland Review:* "Sleeping in the Rain." *Sweet Tree Review:* "Grandma's Baby Grand." *THAT Literary Review:* "In His Image." *Twyckenham Notes:* "Fetal Movements." *Whale Road Review:* "First Christmas." *Wilderness House Literary Review:* "Passing Cars."

CONTENTS

I

Sleeping in the Rain / 1
Easter Sunday / 2
Voices / 3
Requiem for Heavenly Mountain Road / 4
Fathers / 5
SIDS / 6
Rain on the Fourth of July / 7
Fetal Movements / 8
Hives / 9
At the KU Cancer Center / 10
Test Results / 11
Ultrasound with Emergency Volta / 12
At the Independence Women's Clinic / 13
Timetables / 14
Corona / 15
In His Image / 16

II

Poem Written During a Funeral Service / 18
Grandma's Baby Grand / 19
Sandman / 21
Phaedo / 22
Waiting / 23

Unwritten Letter / 24
Housefly / 26
Going Ahead / 27
Crickets / 28
Praying Mantis / 29
Passing Cars / 30
Apnea / 31

III

Still Birth / 34
Wind Chill / 36
Black Ice / 37
Rooming In / 38
Mansions / 39
Grasp Reflex / 40
Halloween / 41
First Christmas / 42
Broken Lights / 43
Sleep Regression / 44
Centipedes / 45
Reading / 46
A City on a Hill / 47

for my son, Theodore

Nicodemus saith unto him, How can a man be born when he is old? can he enter the second time into his mother's womb, and be born?

—John 3:4 (KJV)

FATHER ME AGAIN

I

Sleeping in the Rain

How many inches, if not feet, of August
rain have collected at the algae-green
bottom of the garbage can?

Presumed dead, the supine cicada,
waterlogged in the driveway,
wakes up screaming at the rim of the Mason jar.

My fingers nudge the white petals
of the rosebud—a Japanese beetle stirs
out of deep sleep. I wake up

several times a day, the thumb of God pressing down
on me, its weight extending, writes my radiologist,
along the right corticospinal tract.

Easter Sunday

Pressing my eyeballs, I see star clusters,
microorganisms, a dark tree
standing on the surface of the sun.
I see my wife without me, breastfeeding.

Waking up with a headache in early
morning dark, I wonder: What is
this particular pain? Please,
let it be anything besides the obvious.

If I could just lie here and listen to the rain,
if I could just lie here beside her
breathing, maybe these thunderheads
would roll their stones away.

Voices

> *Not that you could endure*
> *God's voice—far from it. But listen to the voice of the wind*
> *And the ceaseless message that forms itself out of silence.*
>
> —Rainer Maria Rilke

When I listen to the voice of the wind
instead of God's, I hear
a hiss in the oak leaves like rice
pouring into an empty pot.
It makes sense that I would be alone
during the seizure in which I swallow
my tongue, unable to call anyone
to roll over my body,
that I'd be alone during the eclipse
and voiceless in the silence of swallows
flown home from the soybean fields,
alone when my shadow rolls back into my body,
and a chill slips like black lace
into the wind.

Requiem for Heavenly Mountain Road

We can so easily ... find that we are trapped, as in a dream and die there, without ever waking up.
—Rainer Maria Rilke

In a factory park on the outskirts
of Yantai, I would walk around talking
to God: Father, who art in heaven.
And you, my earthly father, I walked

along Heavenly Mountain Road
with you, talking to the charcoal sky.
While you texted one of six women,
I spoke to the windbreaks, the dark

winter tide. Like Rilke I feared
I wasn't really living, and on the night
of my first seizure, I knew I had to die
to bring you back to my bedside.

But Dad, I weary of waiting: If you aren't
coming, I will take your place
at the kitchen counter. I will pick
the paper jackets off cloves of garlic, slice

onion and scoop the seeds out of spaghetti
squash. I will feed your family
in your stead.

I will feed your godforsaken children.

Fathers

A hummingbird stays for a moment
among the zinnias. Then zips
off across the lawn. Soft air brushes
my eyelids, dry lips whispering
words of departure. How can I desire

to be fathered, for my father to come back
and father me again, imagine the bereavement
of my unborn son, his 144 beats per minute?
Clouds converge on the last day in July, closing up
like a scar around the light of this world.

A good steward, I watch over the garden.
Tomatoes redden behind the rusted chain links
of my childhood, twists of wire bent
in the ecstatic race of being
whatever I imagine.

SIDS

Clouds pile overhead like dirty linens, a pillow held
over the blue mouth of heaven. It happens

more often to boys born in the winter. It happens,
again and again, in my imagination:

a dandelion strangled in pea gravel, the *psst!*
of dead cicadas. A hiss of steam escapes

the silver lip of the kettle. But I'm too deep asleep,
burying his body with my own.

Rain on the Fourth of July

Rain prickles the tar-sutured
stomach of the cul-de-sac, burbling
in the curb. My little brother,
orphaned by biological and adoptive
fathers, talks of nothing but fire-
works, and there's no one but me to walk him
and his 30 dollars through the mush
of red paper and empty cartridges to the tent
in the Price Chopper parking lot.
In my black rain jacket, I take note of warning
labels, a counselor at the altar of military
smoke, black snakes and snapdragons, block-
busters in cellophane, torn boxes
of Magnum Pistol Poppers.

Fetal Movements

> *Now faith is the substance of things*
> *hoped for, the evidence of things not seen.*
> —Hebrews 11:1

The unseen rolls over the wall
of her womb, pressing

into the palm of my hand as if it knew
my touch in the dark water.

I see her stomach redden, branch
with blue veins like Burr Oak Woods

at sunset, but I can only count
the kicks, flutters and rolling waves,

symphonic movements of the invisible
world within her. Within me, a sun

is always setting over dark branches,
cirri rifting like the stretchmarks

upon her celestial dome.

Hives

In the waiting room at Saint Luke's Imaging,
Mom watches Hurricane Irma flail Florida's side.

In the machine, my catheter slides an icicle
of contrast dye into my arm.

A sneeze rises in my nostrils
like the flames of a prairie fire. *Lay still,*

says the voice of God over the intercom.
I obey. A needlepoint of beestings stitches itchy

stigmata into my side.
Despite the Benadryl and methylprednisolone,

                      red clouds drift across my scalp.

At First Watch Café, I peel off the co-bind.
Wash the wine stain of blood out of my Mother's eyes.

At the KU Cancer Center

In the waiting room where I pilgrimage myself
to be weighed and blood-pressure
cuffed, pulse-oxed and body-temped
once every four months, Lili nudges
my arm and points to her belly
without a word, as though he were listening

and might stop if he heard us. In the exam room,
she sits on table paper while the nurse
of my oncologist tells me to follow
her finger with my eyes, her finger drawing
the invisible lines of a star or the sign
of the cross. Her hands waggle right and then left,

left and then right, to test my peripheral
vision. Feeling new strength
in my palsied arm, I wrap my hand
around her fingers and pull, pull, pull her
toward me. Push, push, push her away.

Test Results

Enhancement is the leakiness of blood
vessels, the back yard ark
hammered out of 2X4s to raise a garden
above the dogs, a garden of tomato
plants and zinnias, brimming
with dirt, a term in which I slip
on my garden gloves
and loosen the white vermiculate roots.

FLAIR is inflammation, clouds inflamed
at sunset, wafting like torches
over the rooftops. It's the swelling of cherry
tomatoes, the skins that split
if left too long to ripen, the stretchmarks
on Lili's belly.

Tumor infiltrates the brain substance means
I'm as much it as I am
me, as much the man who has affairs
and abandons his children
as the one who stays to steady them.

Ultrasound With Emergency Volta

Gray wisps of cloud slip through the orchard's esbat
of crab apple trees, slinking like wolves

along the white wall of the horizon. Crickets rasp
in the collapsed flowerbed, the torn-down carnival tent

of mid-September, scraping their forewings
together like knives.

Because the baby in her belly isn't growing, I stand
rain-pricked in the driveway.

Because the baby in her belly isn't
growing, I wait in the hospital of autumn rain.

Dying men don't deserve to have children. Dying men
deserve to die.

At the Independence Women's Clinic

Slick and muscular as a tongue
in the jaw, my son
stretches, outgrowing his bag of waters.
Tattooed men walk in, wearing flipflops
and wife-beaters, desert
prophets with dreadlocks and ballcaps.
Their wives and girlfriends stroke full bellies
in mood lighting
dimmer-switched among the fibrous
ceiling panels. Waterlilies shoulder gilded frames,
potted yuccas standing sentry. Below my hand,
the Son of Man rolls over the lining
of her womb like a tongue, mouthing
the Word made flesh.

Timetables

She undresses from the waist down, wraps
her bare bottom in an apron.
When the nurse asks her to hop up
on the table, she heaves
her stomach, the nosecone of a carrier plane.

Her feet lift into the stirrups.
                                        How needless
the nurses were those first few mornings I leapt
from my second bed behind the steel door
of St. Luke's radiation chamber.
My 30 doses, like these 40 weeks, flew by.

Afterwards I hobbled like an octogenarian, leaning
on the girl I married.
Lili walked me back to the lobby, her hand
cupping my elbow.
                                Now she may not make it back
for another visit. After the exam, she swings her legs
over the table's edge. I offer her my hand.

Corona

Speeding away from the clouds
over Arrow Rock, we turn off HWY EE
onto the dirt of 130th Road
and climb into a ditch to witness the eclipse
we would have missed in Arrow Rock,
Columbia or Saint Joseph, the swallows
we would not have seen whisk
above the soybean fields before leaving us
to stand before the shrinking yellow
eyelash of the sun.

       Effacement
refers to Lili's cervix thinning in the soft light,
a tenderness in the tissues
of the wind, relaxing into the reprieve
between contractions, and how easy it is
to see the dark blot as a bite taken,
and grieve the loss of a past life.

After the last dot of sunlight vanishes,
I peel off the paper glasses and gaze
unabashedly upon the ring of blue flames.
Dilation, the head of our newborn,
the moon that overshadows us.

In His Image

> *So God created man in his [own] image, in the image of God created he him; male and female created he them.*
>
> —Genesis 1:27

He's looking over at Dad, says the ultrasound tech.
Darkness and light
shift on screen, the turn of a head.

This white line is his thigh bone, she says
and dots it, mapping his body like treasure chest.
She presses the transducer

into Lili's lower abdomen and snatches
the living image
of God or us? The white glob

of his cheek, flower petal of his penis, the finger
in his nose is his own, not mine.
It is his body that shines
in the dark water.

II

Poem Written During a Funeral Service

The English Department's wired-glass window is dark,
a note tacked to the door:

> *Closed for services of Michelle Boisseau.*

Footsteps echo over the cracked and scuff-marked granite
blocks in which fluorescent bulbs represent themselves
as watery rectangles of light, their geometric
perfection skewed,
a failed mimesis in the mausoleum of art.

The only sound is the whirr of the leaf-blower
a man is walking along the hedgerow. The wind he carries
upends a mountain ridge of fallen leaves.

Air erupts with the lava of leaves, an underwater volcano.
Elephant grass undulates like anemone
in the drowning sky. I hear a voice in the clouds,
kindergarteners or geese I cannot tell.

    Classmates walk by with their heads down.

Grandma's Baby Grand

Charles Friend drags the dusting brush
of his vacuum cleaner over the tuning pins
below the lid of Grandma's baby grand,
a 1929 Wurlitzer in which dust
collects like ash from the smokestack

of a crematorium. He pulls back
on the tennis ball handle of his tuning
wrench, like he's changing gears in a stick
shift with one hand while pounding
the one key with the other
like a migraine that the house is having.

    On the day that
the moving van carrying her baby
grand turned onto our cul-de-sac, Grandma
told the driver he had the wrong address,
he should take it back to Independence.

    Mr. Friend says
every piano has a memory, its own unique set
of overtones. Grandma could not remember
burning the bacon or pouring her husband bowls
of chicken soup congealed over weeks

on the stovetop. She forgot about driving the wrong
way down I-70, but I remember her liver-spotted
hands on the keys, playing *My Way*
until the sheets vanished, and then the notes.
And the lyrics.

Sandman

I crawl through the grass
dappled leaf light of crab apple trees.
I crawl into the ribcage of my unborn son's
crib. Sawdust stings my eyes

like sleepiness, particles that the mouse
scratches out of the slats, the sand
that is sprinkled into the eyes
of the dreamer. The palm sander

buzzes below my hand and in it, conducting
static to my fingertips, the tingling
of an arm that goes to sleep
because I am asleep, and lying on it,

the arm that stays numb because of nerve
damage from the seizure, what the nurses call
residual, or *deficit*, a droopiness
in the left side of my face.

Phaedo

My dog mouths the tennis ball like a syllable
in black gums, the first syllable
of a poem I am writing about playing catch
with my dog, Phaedo.

Leaf mulch and hay catch in his winter coat.
I snatch the ball out of his mouth
and fling its smudged neon
nap into sunlight. Phaedo belongs to me

the way we belong to the gods, says Socrates.
Men are possessions, our bodies a kind of prison,
a chain-link fence, and the gods mind
the gates. The gods mind me, my tennis ball

leaping in the faded grass. I know my life
does not belong to me. I know I must chase down
the days of my life and ever so reluctantly
lay them at my master's feet.

Waiting

> *After such painstaking study of empty-gate dharma,*
> *... there's nothing left but that old poetry demon.*
>
> —Po Chü-i

In cold October wind, I wake up with an extra blanket
over my feet. Sunday morning clouds
scud across the western sky,

going somewhere in a hurry.
                        The grass remembers yesterday's
paintbrushes, their rinse and stain,

a lower back ache. My wife waits for me to finish
writing, for her labor
to come naturally. I hear her chopping

in the kitchen of my brain, stir-fries for the freezer,
working hard to give herself a break.
                        Sunrise cuts my shadow
over the whitewashed grass. It's always the same with me.
Trying to empty myself, I fill another page.

Unwritten Letter

—for Michelle Boisseau

Because you had cancer and I had cancer,
you put your arms around me,
Mother of poems. You put your arms around me
in a banquet hall. Because I had cancer

and you had cancer, we recognized each other.
In a crowd, we sat at the same table,
discussing diets: me, going ketogenic, you going
with the green sludge your guru

concocted to counteract the glasses of red.
Your students called you sergeant, as I would
and follow you, Michelle. I know one day
I must, because you dropped f-bombs

in the name of Poetry and though I find myself today
once more among the living, I put on my blues
for you, Michelle, my blue jeans and T-shirt
V-necked like the flock of geese I hear faintly honking.

Sky blue I am for you, cirrus-chalked and shadow-lined.
Why does my heart beat while yours does not?
The pin oak shushes me, and I suffer myself to be quiet.
Listen to the poetry of that one breath the world

heaves overhead and all around me. Hell, yes, Michelle.
I'll raise a ruckus. Write your vigor.
Write your sex. Sing and singe in the threadbare seam
between being and being gone.

Housefly

A housefly jitters in sunlight against the storm
door to my study. *He's leaving,* she says
in an email I opened but did not bother to read.
You used to know him. Would you have called this?

Before I know what is happening, I'm writing
a treatise of hindsight and warning signs, all the things
I've held back over the years, not wanting
to presume. After all, who was I to have an opinion?

A childhood ghost. But now it's all so very present.
I'm going back to revisit the gypsy
he chased at the Renaissance Fair, looking at Facebook
photos in a new light. I think about opening

the door, fetching the flyswatter.
Saint Benedict says not to kill and not to commit adultery
are instruments of good works. Also,
to see death before me daily, I must examine myself

in the light of a dying star, the light my fly sponges
off the glass

before a spider wraps her legs around his shoulders
and softly kisses his neck.

Going Ahead

I sit in the sanctuary of shade
and stirring leaves. Down the road,
an elderly man cleaves
to his handrail like a child
taking his first step into the deep end.

His wife's caretaker carts her
to the curb ahead of him
and starts the engine. A yellow leaf
falls out of the crab apple tree
into the green lap of my thirtieth year.

In the end, he pushes the empty chair back
up the walk and leaves it on the stoop.
Its chrome armrests catch the sun,
constellating needle
points of light.

Crickets

Among the living things I've killed
I count the one I flushed,
the one I hit with the head of a broom
in the furnace room at midnight.

I couldn't watch the bumblebee
beat itself to death inside the Mason jar,
and I memorialized the brown
garden snake. Mom and I dropped the vole

in the dumpster, not a pot
of boiling water. Nevertheless, oak leaves
and spider webs collect in the chimney
corner of the back yard, gathering

behind the cement rabbit with one broken ear
the evidence of autumn. The dead
press their case against me.

Praying Mantis

A chill of long-awaited autumn air
infiltrates the stillness of a praying mantis
the color of fallen leaves
crouched among fallen leaves.

I swipe the seat of the lawn chair
left out overnight to condense water
out of the dark. A startled cicada sputters
among dead zinnias. Beyond the trees
a garbage truck gasps in the joints of its pistons.

A chainsaw squeals. When the praying mantis
comes out of its trance, glass intervenes
between it and wet grass, holding the world
apart, as in an out-of-body experience.

It sees but cannot reach the lawn.
I see my loved ones gathered
around a hospital bed. Its raptorial forelegs
ping off the surface of the green beyond.

Passing Cars

—in memory of Peter Bonnefin

When I unlock and lift up on the brass
handle of the window to my study,
the southwestern breath of autumn's end
goes mouth-to-mouth with me
at the lip of windowsill, the breeze stirring

tattered cobwebs in the tracks
of the upper sash. The body of a housefly
turns over in its sleep. My cousin, Erin,
on the redeye to Sydney hears him
say it's all right and wakes up, too late

to say goodbye. On the last day
of autumn, the AC is silent. I listen
to the traffic for reassurance. Cars passing
beyond the mossy pickets heave
like the souls of the departed.

Apnea

noun, Pathology.
1. a temporary suspension
of breathing, occurring in some newborns.

In the early morning dark
where I walk, it sounds as if the whole world
is holding its breath, waiting
for a squirrel to pick itself up and walk away
from its body and brains
dashed along the street, prostrate,
I-70 murmuring like a lamasery
beyond the rooftops. The interstate tosses
in its rocky bed, all the contrivances
of man. Oak leaves choke
the storm drain. No one is coming
to clean up the mess.

III

Still Birth

Nigh, nigh
in the labor room,
you doze between contractions.

I grow faint, offering sips
of water from a Styrofoam cup.
Push! Push! Push!

Dr. Moreno screams, perched
between your legs,
her gloved finger hooked
in your vagina like the mouth of a fish.

Hour after hour,
after hour.

Then black hair
appears in the mirror
angled for you to see
into the stretched
and bloody lips of the birth canal.

With one final push, he flops out,
stillborn
purple, extraterrestrial

conehead, vernix
crumbling on his skin
like cottage cheese.

Apgar of three, bathed in the blood
of a split perineum,
he hesitates.

I hold my breath. I dare not
breathe.

Lili asks where he is, *where is my baby.*
My eyes burn, brimming

with saltwater. Beached,
I am as still as he is.

Wind Chill

Downstream from the Quad Cities Generating Station,
a train of steam rolls over the surface
of the Mississippi. At four below zero,
the wind is chill as a razorblade on my tongue,
a communion wafer of high carbon steel.
I walk with my collar pulled up and my head
held down, my face held together
as if broken in gloved hands.

Wind pushes clumps of snow off branches
and in midair they disintegrate into particles
of diamond glass. I cannot see the water
below the rolling conflagration of its conflict
with the air, its long train of ghostly flames
lifting off Moline. Only I am out walking today
above my uncle's house, strings of geese draped
overhead like prayer beads.

Black Ice

Snow beards the wheel wells, drapes white pelts

over the roof of the car, the lid

                of the COUNTY DISPOSAL can.

Black ice on the back patio, pawprints pointing
in every direction,

snow fills the mouth

of the birdbath. Dark green blades break
through the cloak of snow, aching

                for daylight. Awakened insects,

once awake, cannot go back to sleep.

In the passenger seat, I whisk by a woman
walking through a snowbank,

gray tank top stretched over her full belly.

Rooming In

While our week-old son lies
skewed under the lights of the Bili-bassinet,
nurses squeeze black beads of blood
from his heel. Lili and I room in a dream
she dreams of her uncle on a bus
on fire and all the passengers burnt except for their clothes.

When they get off at a stop to say goodbye to their families,
Lili hides in a rack of clothes. The bus turns
into a crate, a shipping container,

and it drives into the lake, the passengers partying:
those who can sing,
sing; those who can recite,
recite and finger-paint the corrugated walls
of the sinking room.

Twitching in the aquarium-blue lights of the Bili-bassinet,
our son twists, *Now I Lay Me Down To Sleep* plastered
above the venetian blinds of the Isolation Room,
the warm chamber of God knows
what a newborn dreams.

Mansions

Lying in, Lili breastfeeds, her deflated belly
puffing below the newborn
in her arms. My estranged father
threatens to toss us out on the street.

Time to hunker down for winter, clip
the year's last blossom
from the rosebush
and prop it upright in a jar.

In the witchy bramble of crab apple
branches, the martin's house rocks, cable
anchored to bough. Suspended
between heaven and earth, we sit

in the sunroom on a cloudy day.
All the birds have gone away.

Grasp Reflex

The bright cold blue green of this world
glazes over your gray eyes
at the windowpane. What the world is to you is
what I am to you
because you can see no farther than my face.

When you cry, you cry because the bright
cold blue green
of me is too much for you. I shush you like wind.

I lie down next to you and stroke your palm
until your tiny fingers
open and all five of your fingers
close around the tip
of one of my mine because I am huge.

You cannot imagine how big I am.

Halloween

Because of my October at the Department of Radiology,
the UMKC School of Dentistry turned me away
for a free screening. Because of my October
at the Department of Radiology, I developed pneumonia
from a head cold, and Urgent Care sent me to the emergency
room. Because of my October at the Department

of Radiology, my favorite holiday is Halloween
when the zombies of tomato plants rot at their stakes
and oak leaves unspindle from a spiral of branches, falling
head over heels to cowlick and constellate the yellow grass.
On Halloween I pause over the moon's wounded gibbous,
the garden mums and pumpkins racked outside Walmart.

I love the throb of gaslights, the one red lamp
burning in the bay window of the abandoned house.
Stars prick the dark because of my October
at the Department of Radiology. Treetops hiss
like a breath sucked through clenched teeth.

First Christmas

Green grass bristles below the snow.
Crows walk the lawn, undertakers
in their black suits. Blue jays descend
upon the back patio to peck at dog food.

Under the wind's constant surveillance,
I walk to the lip of the cul-de-sac, the edge
of my confine, slush splashed over the curbside.

I need to stretch my legs below the oak leaves,
brown rags hanging in the charcoal sky.
Rock salt burns holes in the history of the ice,
yesterday's bootprints, encrusted.

All I want is for this narrow life to last.

Broken Lights

Smashed into chunks
of ice, the dog
water glows in morning dark.
A blue jay flips into the oak
and speaks, its shriek
one of the few birdsongs I know,
the one that goes, I'm here, are you there?

When he wakes up to find himself alone,
the same scream comes
from his bedroom door, the one that goes:
I thought you were with me,
but when I woke up you were gone

and now I don't know what to do
because I, too, have woken up
to find myself forsaken
on a dark winter morning, guided only
by the light of my own
brokenness.

Sleep Regression

Unlearning sleep, my infant son wakes up
seven times a night.

I stumble like a drunk
in the dark. I hoist him into my arms.

In the bathroom mirror, we size each other up—

The Velcro wings of his swaddle dangle
at his side, his tiny hands clasped
before a wellspring of drool, the fountainhead
of his chin, as if in supplication, a sinner
in the hands of an angry god.

We stare at one another. His dark eyes meet mine.

Goddammit, his dark eyes *are* mine.

Centipedes

The legs of a centipede whisk across the ceiling.

Its legs bat like eyelashes above my baby boy.

Morning storms dim like cataracts in the glass

bricks of the window well. Because we live

underground, I imagine my son one day

will put a centipede in his mouth.

One day I picked up a knot of Lili's hair

and a shock shot through my fingertips.

I pulled back my hand.

A centipede fell out. At the edge of the sky

blue play mat, Larry the Koala stares out of his black

marble eyes. Zoey the Zebra sits beside him

with hers sewn shut. Thunderheads trundle

over the rooftop. My son chomps down,

gumming a small toy truck.

Reading

Craned neck, head raised
high above Lili's clavicle to fasten his eyes
upon mine because I am reading,
the reading is coming from me, he answers with *Oh!*
forming the vowel whole
in his tiny toothless mouth. He says oh the way we do,
as if for the first time understanding

this thing called reading, this human technology
of eyes and mouths. How we lift our voices.
His eyes move from mine to the page where mine are looking.
Then they move back to me and I raise my eyes
from the page and now we're looking into each other's eyes
for the first time. His big toothless smile
makes me smile with the dry saline burn of pure joy.

A City on a Hill

> *Ye are the light of the world. A city that is set on an hill cannot be hid.*
>
> —Matthew 5:14

Lying on the bed, I suffer no confusion.
No visual or cognitive changes imply
that my glioblastoma has exhausted its local
blood supply and marched highways
of white matter to rape the other towns
in my brain.
                     Winter light enters the glass
bricks above my bed and scatterfires
into the wall where stalks of lightning rise
and cords fall, as if to link the exploding city
of light with its power source.
                               I lie in bed,
watching a rainbow blown to smithereens
on the wall I painted *Heavenly Blue*
for a newborn. His name is Theodore, *Theo*
from the Greek meaning God and *dore,*

a gift of, a gift from whom these months have come
I do not know. Glioblastoma,
glioblastoma,
                            glioblastoma,

blow me open,   take me home.

Cameron Morse lives with his wife Lili and son Theodore in Blue Springs, Missouri. He was diagnosed with a glioblastoma in 2014. With a 14.6 month life expectancy, he entered the Creative Writing program at the University of Missouri—Kansas City and, in 2018, graduated with an M.F.A. His poems have been published in over 100 different magazines, including *New Letters, Bridge Eight, South Dakota Review, I-70 Review* and *TYPO*. His first collection, *Fall Risk*, won Glass Lyre Press's 2018 Best Book Award.

This project was made possible, in part, by generous support from the Osage Arts Community.

Osage Arts Community provides temporary time, space and support for the creation of new artistic works in a retreat format, serving creative people of all kinds — visual artists, composers, poets, fiction and nonfiction writers. Located on a 152-acre farm in an isolated rural mountainside setting in Central Missouri and bordered by ¾ of a mile of the Gasconade River, OAC provides residencies to those working alone, as well as welcoming collaborative teams, offering living space and workspace in a country environment to emerging and mid-career artists. For more information, visit us at www.osageac.org

www.ingramcontent.com/pod-product-compliance
Lightning Source LLC
Chambersburg PA
CBHW021451080526
44588CB00009B/800